A FRIEND IN THE LIBRARY

LIBRARY

HUMOR

BY

EVA MARCH TAPPAN

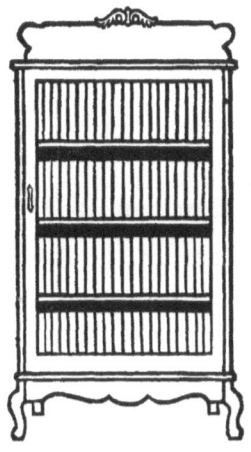

British Library Cataloguing-in-Publication Data
A catalogue record for this book is available from the
British Library

HUMOR

A FRIEND IN THE LIBRARY

A Practical Guide to the Writings of

RALPH WALDO EMERSON
NATHANIEL HAWTHORNE
HENRY WADSWORTH LONGFELLOW
JAMES RUSSELL LOWELL
JOHN GREENLEAF WHITTIER
OLIVER WENDELL HOLMES

IN TWELVE VOLUMES
VOLUME VI

Eva March Tappan

Eva March Tappan was born on 26th December 1854 in Blackstone, Massachusetts, America. She is well known as a factual as well as fictional writer, but spent her early career as a teacher. Tappan was the only child of Reverend Edmund March Tappan and Lucretia Logée, and received her education at the esteemed Vassar College. This was a private coeducational liberal arts college, in the town of Poughkeepsie, New York, from which she graduated in 1875. Here, Tappan was a member of Phi Beta Kappa, the oldest honour society for the liberal arts and sciences, widely considered as the nations most prestigious society. She also edited the *Vassar Miscellany*, a college publication.

After leaving her early education, Tappan began teaching at Wheaton College, one of the oldest institutions of higher education for women in the United States, founded in 1834 and based in Norton, Massachusetts. She taught Latin and German here, from 1875 until 1880, before moving on to the Raymond Academy in Camden, New Jersey where she was associate Principal until 1894. Tappan also received a graduate degree in English Literature from the University of Pennsylvania. This allowed her to pursue her first love, that of reading and writing, and she taught as head of the English department at the English High School at Worcester, Massachusetts.

It was only after this date that Tappan began her literary career, writing about famous characters in history, often aimed at educating children in important historical themes and epochs. Some of her better known works include, *In the Days of William the Conqueror* (1901) and *In the Days of Queen Elizabeth* (1902), *The Out-of-Door Book* (1907), *When Knights Were Bold* (1911) and *The Little Book of the Flag* (1917). Tappan never married, being a happy singleton, and died on 29th January 1930, aged seventy-five.

HUMOR

A SENSE of humor is an exceedingly good quality to possess. Like the pig of the cotter, it is "a mighty convenient thing to have in the house." It brightens a dull time, it throws sunshine upon troublesome questions, and it clears the air. Lowell says that a sense of humor is a "modulating and restraining balance-wheel" ("Democracy," vii. 1). Most certainly the man with a keen appreciation of humor is saved from a good many blunders, because he can see how ridiculous they would make him. He cannot very well be unduly elated by any small success, because, knowing how many greater successes there are in the world, he realizes the absurdity of being puffed up by a little one. He cannot take himself half so seriously as the humorless man, for he sees how ridiculous it is to fancy that his acts and opinions are of preëminent value in a world containing so many millions of people. Often, instead of getting angry with the one who opposes him, the man with a sense of humor cannot help smiling at some ludicrous aspect of the situation; and in most conflicts the man who can smile is reasonably sure to win.

There are various kinds of so-called humorous writings, and some of them contain not a line of either humor or wit. The only excuse for laughing at the silly "jokes" of the "funny page" is that laughing at them may have become an uncontrollable nervous habit. It is fortunate if the paragraphs are only silly and not distinctly pernicious. I have just taken up at random two numbers of a well-known daily paper, not a "yellow journal" by any means, but a paper with strong, wise editorials and excellent book reviews, a paper that has never failed to be on the right side in any reform of the day; but look at the mental food which it provides for the lover of humor! In these two numbers there is the ancient story of the boy who asks permission to attend his grandmother's funeral when he really wants to go to a ball-game. There is the youth who tells the girl under the mistletoe that he wants to kiss her "so as to get acquainted." There is the husband who has the happiest time of his life when his wife cannot use her voice for a while. And this is the way that an intelligent family newspaper teaches truthfulness, respect for age, modesty, and regard for the sacredness of home-life! It is small wonder that foreigners are inclined to scoff at "American humor," — and it is as fair to take such abominable stuff for a sample of our best humor as it would be to take Mother Goose for a sample of our best poetry.

The year 1846 is famous in the history of American humor as the date of Lowell's "Biglow Papers" (x. xi). Lowell was an earnest supporter of the anti-slavery cause, and in the belief that the Mexican War had been brought about to strengthen the slave power, he wrote the "Biglow Papers." They are introduced as written by one Hosea Biglow, who is a parishioner of the learned Parson Wilbur. The humor of them begins with the first sentence of the preface. In this Lowell says he has observed the custom of collecting favorable notices of books to use in publishing a second edition, and it occurs to him that it would be economical and convenient to prepare them himself and to prefix them to the first edition, for, he says, "to delay attaching the *bobs* until the second attempt at flying the kite would indicate but a slender experience in that useful art." Then he manufactures the most comical parody of "book-reviews" that can be imagined, purporting to come from the "Universal Littery Universe," the "Higginbottomopolis Snapping-Turtle," and others.

Lowell chose to write in the Yankee dialect, the talk which he heard as a boy at "noonings" in his father's hay-fields; and it is worth while to read at least enough of his introduction to find out that many of the so-called Yankeeisms are found in the standard authors of the sixteenth century or earlier.

One of the best of the " Biglow Papers " is the speech of the candidate (x. 136) who cares for nothing but votes, and is terribly afraid of losing any by "committing himself."

> Ez to my princerples, I glory
> In hevin' nothin' o' the sort;
> I ain't a Wig, I ain't a Tory,
> I'm jest a canderdate, in short.

On the question of war, this "canderdate" expresses himself as follows: —

> Ez fer the war, I go agin' it, —
> I mean to say I kind o' du, —
> Thet is, I mean thet, bein' in it,
> The best way wuz to fight it thru;

HUMOR

Not but wut abstract war is horrid,
I sign to thet with all my heart,
But civlyzation *doos* get forrid
Sometimes upon a powder-cart.

The "Biglow Papers" were so entirely different from any of Lowell's previous writings that at first no one supposed him to be their author. Indeed, he had the pleasure of listening while it was positively proved — to the satisfaction of the speaker — that he could not possibly have written them. He saw them pinned up in workshops and copied everywhere, and he was almost startled to find what a power lay in his hands.

During the Civil War, Lowell brought out a second series of "Biglow Papers." These are full of bits of wisdom that did not lose their value with the coming of peace. At the time of the capture of Mason and Slidell, he wrote two poems. From the first, a talk between the Concord Bridge and the Bunker Hill Monument (x. 128), come such sayings as, —

Hard work is good an' wholesome, past all doubt;
But 't ain't so, ef the mind gits tuckered out.

Don't never prophesy — onless ye know.

Now don't go off half-cock: folks never gains
By usin' pepper-sauce instid o' brains.

She's riled jes' now. — Plain proof her cause ain't
    strong, —
The one that fust gits mad's 'most allers wrong.

Folks never understand the folks they hate.

Folks thet worked thorough was the ones thet **thriv,**
But bad work follers ye ez long 's ye live;
You can't git red on 't; jest ez sure ez sin,
It's allers askin' to be done agin.

HUMOR

Lowell closes with his fine stanza beginning, —

O strange New World, thet yit wast never young.

His second poem, written at this time, was the well known " Jonathan to John" (x. 141).

> It don't seem hardly right, John,
> When both my hands was full,
> To stump me to a fight, John, —
> Your cousin, tu, John Bull.

Such are the "Biglow Papers," full of humor and keen satire and bits of practical wisdom, but with every now and then a fervent outburst of patriotism.

Another poem, always printed with the "Biglow Papers," a delightful idyl of Yankeedom, is "The Courtin'" (xi. 80), wherein,

> Zekle crep' up quite unbeknown
> An' peeked in thru the winder,

An' there sot Huldy all alone,
'ith no one nigh to hender, —

which Lowell declares he wrote to fill a blank page and accommodate the publisher.

In Lowell's prose there is a constant play of humor, — his letters especially are running over with it, — but it so depends upon the context that it is as difficult to quote it as to photograph a gleam of the northern lights. He does not often allow humor to enter a serious poem, but he never bars the door of his prose to it, no matter on what subject he is writing. In a critical essay on Chaucer (ii. 183), he queries, "Should a man discover the art of transmuting metals and present us with a lump of gold as large as an ostrich egg, would it be in human nature to inquire too nicely whether he had stolen the lead?" In

his introduction to the second series of the
"Biglow Papers" (ix. 5), on a page which is
crowded with the results of wide reading and
scholarly thinking, he says, "In one of Dod-
sley's Old Plays we have *onions* rhymed with
minions, — I have tears in my eyes while I
record it." On another page of equal learning
("Library of Old Authors," ii. 273), he de-
mands, "What shall we say to our editor's
not knowing that *fry* was used formerly where
we should say *burn?* Lovers used to *fry* with
love, whereas now they have got out of the
frying-pan into the fire."

Lowell's "Fable for Critics" (xii. 17) — be
sure to read *aloud* the title page and "To the
Reader" — is of great value as a piece of literary criticism, but it is also immensely amusing
for its puns, and its preposterous rhymes; *irre-*

sistible — whist-table — untwistable — Chris-tabel, are some of them. His hero

> Was never precisely unkind,
> The defect in his brain was just absence of mind.

He was

> A terrible fellow to meet in society,
> Not the toast that he buttered was ever so dry at tea.

In 1857 Lowell was asked to edit the new magazine, the "Atlantic Monthly." He accepted the invitation on condition that Oliver Wendell Holmes would agree to become a contributor. Holmes agreed and sent to the first number a paper which began, "I was just going to say when I was interrupted." The interruption had been twenty-five years long, for in 1832 he had written two articles called "The Autocrat of the Breakfast-Table," and he took the same title for the series that he now began. The scene is laid at a boarding-house table. The Autocrat talks on and on, about novel-writing, horse-racing, poetry, the make-up of the brain, agreeable voices, the front door and the side door to people's feelings, the fragrance of budding lilac-leaves — anything and everything; but he is always bright, witty, and entertaining. At the table is the divinity student, whom the Autocrat allows "to take a certain share in the conversation." There is the landlady; the lady boarder, who has calmly requested "a few original stanzas" for her autograph album; the landlady's daughter, who says "Yes?" wears much jewelry, and reads Byron while her mother makes the puddings; the "young fellow called John"; and the schoolmistress,

who in the closing chapter agrees to walk "the
long path" with the Autocrat. The wise and
witty talk goes on. "It is not easy, at the best,
for two persons talking together to make the
most of each other's thoughts, there are so
many of them," declares the Autocrat.
"When John and Thomas, for instance, are
talking together, it is natural enough that
among the six there should be more or less con-
fusion and misapprehension." The landlady
turns pale, fearing the Autocrat has "a screw
loose" and she will lose a boarder. The old
gentleman opposite slides the carving-knife to
one side, "as it were carelessly." The Autocrat explains: "There is the real John, known
only to his Maker; John's ideal John, never
the real one, and often very unlike him;
Thomas's ideal John, never the real John, nor

John's John, but often very unlike either. In like manner there are three Thomases." The Autocrat adds in brackets: —

A very unphilosophical application of the above remarks was made by a young fellow answering to the name of John, who sits near me at table. A certain basket of peaches, a rare vegetable, little known to boarding-houses, was on its way to me *via* this unlettered Johannes. He appropriated the three that remained in the basket, remarking that there was just one apiece for him. I convinced him that his practical inference was hasty and illogical, but in the mean time he had eaten the peaches.

"The Autocrat" was followed by "The Professor" (ii.) and "The Poet" (iii.). The three books are sparkling with bright sayings, such as, —

Knowledge and timber should n't be much used till they are seasoned.

If you have the consciousness of genius, do something to show it.

Truth is tough. It will not break like a bubble, at a touch; nay, you may kick it about all day, like a football, and it will be round and full at evening.

Put not your trust in money, but put your money in trust.

There is the famous paragraph beginning, "Our brains are seventy-year clocks" (i. 185), the equally famous one contrasting the mountains and the sea (i. 264); there are poems, "The Deacon's Masterpiece, or The Wonderful One-Hoss Shay," and "The Chambered Nautilus" among them. There is the story of Iris (ii. 60); there is the picture of the ship and the "little toiling steam-tug" that is doing all the work of pulling it along (ii. 289). Everywhere in the three books there is plenty of humor.

HUMOR

Even in his medical lectures Holmes can no more leave out the gleam of humor than he can stop breathing. "I know there are professors in this country who 'ligate' arteries," he says ("Scholastic and Bedside Teaching," ix. 273). "Other surgeons only tie them, and it stops the bleeding just as well." Again, "A man is not a plant, or, at least, he is a very curious one, for he carries his soil in his stomach, which is a kind of portable flower-pot, and he grows round it, instead of out of it" ("Border Lines in Medical Science," ix. 209).

Holmes has written many verses that are witty and amusing; but far superior to these are the poems whose fun only clears the way for some noble thought. In "The Old Man Dreams" (xii. 295), an old man begs the listening angel for but one hour of his youth again. The angel asks if the years have brought him nothing that he would be sorry to lose. He bethinks himself and replies:—

> Ah, truest soul of womankind!
>   Without thee what were life?
> One bliss I cannot leave behind:
>   I'll take — my — precious — wife!

Again the angel asks the question, and he begs for his girl and boys.

> The smiling angel dropped his pen, —
>   "Why, this will never do;
> The man would be a boy again,
>   And be a father too!"

This is rather different humor from the vulgar story of the man whose happiest hour was the one in which his wife could not talk to him.

Best of all Holmes's poems of humor is

Lincoln's favorite, "The Last Leaf" (xii. 3). The "last leaf" was an old man, said to have been one of the "Indians" of the Boston Tea-party, who in Holmes's boyhood used to appear in the Boston streets "in his cocked hat and knee-breeches, with his buckled shoes and his sturdy cane." Holmes writes with honest tenderness, —

> The mossy marbles rest
> On the lips that he has prest
> In their bloom,
> And the names he loved to hear
> Have been carved for many a year
> On the tomb.

But the tear is followed by a smile when the poet says penitently, —

> I know it is a sin
> For me to sit and grin
> At him here;

But the old three-cornered hat,
And the breeches, and all that,
Are so queer !

The poem closes:—

And if I should live to be
The last leaf upon the tree
In the spring,
Let them smile, as I do now,
At the old forsaken bough
Where I cling.

This poem was almost a prophecy, for Holmes outlived Lowell, Hawthorne, Longfellow, Emerson, and Whittier.

In the writings of Emerson Lowell noted the "humor which always played about the horizon of his mind like heat-lightning." No one could have expressed better Emerson's species of humor; for while he has a keen sense of a humorous situation, he never portrays it with the rollicking merriment of Lowell or Holmes. For instance, in speaking of the prophetess Cassandra, who uttered truth, but was fated by the gods never to win belief ("Mary Moody Emerson," x. 397), he says that "Cassandra domesticated in a lady's house would have proved a troublesome boarder." He generally expresses the humorous with a little restraint, almost as if his brilliant, erratic, intensely devoted Aunt Mary Moody Emerson were watching him with her warnings against "folly," as she called any approach to humor. Yet, in his paper, "Mary Moody Emerson" (x. 397), he gives himself freer rein than in any other except the one on Brook Farm. He shows in every paragraph his love and respect for her, but he thoroughly enjoys her oddities. "She had the misfortune of spinning with a greater velocity than any of the other tops," he says; and he tells various amusing stories of her. One was her way of suppressing an inquisitive questioner by demanding abruptly, "How's your cat?" Brook Farm, Emerson describes ("Life and Letters in New England," x. 326) as

A perpetual picnic, a French Revolution in small, an Age of Reason in a patty-pan.

Of course every visitor found that there was a comic side to this Paradise of shepherds and shepherdesses. There was a stove in every chamber, and every one might burn as much wood as he or she would saw. The ladies took cold on washing-day; so it was ordained that the gentlemen-shepherds should wring and hang out the clothes; which they punctually did. And it would sometimes occur that when they danced in the evening, clothes-pins dropped plentifully from their pockets.

HUMOR

Some one tells a story ("Emerson," xii. 464) of hearing Emerson say in a lecture "in his musical and curiously impersonal voice," "If we could only make up our minds always to tell the truth, the whole truth, and nothing but the truth, — to what embarrassing situations it would give rise."

For a man who appreciated humor so keenly it is strange that so little appears in the poems of Whittier. There is fun enough in his rhymed letters to Lucy Larcom (iv. 405, 408).

Believe me, Lucy Larcom, it gives me real sorrow
That I cannot take my carpet-bag and go to town to-
    morrow;
But I'm "snow-bound," and cold on cold, like layers
    of an onion,
Have piled my back and weighed me down as with the
    pack of Bunyan;

and he tosses off the merry little punning poem on Mary Grew (iv. 126), with its changing refrains, —

> To conscience and to duty true,
> So, up from childhood, Mary Grew, —

and —

> The way to make the world anew,
> Is just to grow — as Mary Grew.

His "Double-Headed Snake of Newbury" (i. 192) is full of a whimsical humor. He says slyly, —

> Think what a zest it gave to the sport,
> In berry-time, of the younger sort,
> As over pastures blackberry-twined,
> Reuben and Dorothy lagged behind,
> And closer, closer, for fear of harm,
> The maiden clung to her lover's arm;
> And how the spark, who was forced to stay,
> By his sweetheart's fears, till the break of day,
> Thanked the snake for the fond delay!

Whittier adds a moral to this wonder-tale, but in merrier fashion than the old "This fable teaches" of the Æsop stories.

But of Whittier's humorous writings, "Abram Morison" (ii. 182), a memory of his boyhood's days, is the gayest and cheeriest. It is a picture of the honest Scotch-Irishman who came "wandering down from Nutfield woods" to dwell among the Quaker folk, to delight the older people with his simple honesty and the younger ones with his stories of fairies and goblins, of "witch and troll and second sight," and his quaint fashion of life.

> Back and forth to daily meals,
> Rode his cherished pig on wheels;
> And to all who came to see:
> "Aisier for the pig an' me,
> Sure it is," said Morison.

Heaven forgive the half-checked smile,
Of our careless boyhood,

says the poet, while he recalls the good man's
talk in meeting.

"Don't," he's pleading, "don't ye go,
Dear young friends, to sight and show;
Don't run after elephants,
Learned pigs and presidents,
And the likes!" said Morison.

It is really too bad that a writer who could
bring forth such excellent pieces of humor did
not give us more of it.

Longfellow's best humorous writing is in
"The Courtship of Miles Standish" (ii. 305).
The rough little room in early Plymouth
stands before us as we read, the stripling John
Alden "writing with diligent speed at a table
of pine by the window," while the doughty

Miles Standish paces to and fro and tells of his arms and the good care that he gives them. He says:—

"That's what I always say; if you wish a thing to be
    well done,
You must do it yourself, you must not leave it to
    others!"

The Captain never guessed that in the letters which John Alden was writing, "Every sentence began or closed with the name of Priscilla"; and after a while he said to the young man:—

"Go to the damsel Priscilla, the loveliest maiden of
    Plymouth,
Say that a blunt old Captain, a man not of words but
    of actions,
Offers his hand and his heart, the hand and heart of a
    soldier.
Not in these words, you know, but this in short is my
    meaning.

A FRIEND IN THE LIBRARY

I am a maker of war, and not a maker of phrases.

You, who are bred as a scholar, can say it in elegant
language,

Such as you read in your books of the pleadings and
wooings of lovers,

Such as you think best adapted to win the heart of a
maiden."

Poor John Alden begs the Captain to stand
by his own maxim, but he answers:—

"Truly the maxim is good, and I do not mean to gain-
say it;

But we must use it discreetly, and not waste powder
for nothing.

Now, as I said before, I was never a maker of phrases.

I can march up to a fortress and summon the place to
surrender,

But march up to a woman with such a proposal, I
dare not.

I'm not afraid of bullets, nor shot from the mouth of a
cannon,

But of a thundering 'No!' point-blank from the
    mouth of a woman,
That I confess I'm afraid of, nor am I ashamed to
    confess it!"

Honest John Alden went forth, heart-
broken, but bound to do his best for his
friend.

But as he warmed and glowed, in his simple and elo-
    quent language,
Quite forgetful of self, and full of the praise of his
    rival,
Archly the maiden smiled, and, with eyes overflowing
    with laughter,
Said, in a tremulous voice —

but the climax must be left to Longfellow
himself, and it is almost wicked to tell any of
the story, for no one can do it so well as he.

Hawthorne's humor has a special charm of
its own. Even in his books for children their

is plenty of it. In the story of the Pygmies ("Tanglewood Tales," xiii. 290), and their friendship for the giant Antæus, he makes the tiny folk say in a tone of superiority, "Let us be kind to the old fellow. Why, if Mother Earth had not been very kind to ourselves, we might all have been Giants too." By a political overthrow, Hawthorne was put out of his position in the Custom House. He says of this ("The Custom House," vi.), "Meanwhile the press had taken up my affair, and kept me, for a week or two, careering through the public prints, in my decapitated state, like Irving's Headless Horseman; ghastly and grim and longing to be buried, as a politically dead man ought." Hawthorne might have jested even more gayly than this if he could only have looked ahead a little way; for while another man of different political faith sat at his desk in the Custom House, he was writing "The Scarlet Letter," the book that was to make his fame and literary calling sure. Six months later, he wrote to a friend, "I finished my book only yesterday, one end being in press in Boston, while the other was in my head here in Salem; so that, as you see, the story is at least fourteen miles long." "The House of the Seven Gables" (vii.) is full of humorous touches. Of the false-hearted Judge Pyncheon he says (page 167), the observer might suspect "that the smile on the gentleman's face was a good deal akin to the shine on his boots, and that each must have cost him and his bootblack, respectively, a good deal of hard labor to bring out and preserve them." In another chapter he tells of the visit of a small boy to Hepzibah's little store, who at his previous calls has swallowed a whole gingerbread menagerie.

Phœbe, on entering the shop, beheld there the already familiar face of the little devourer — if we can reckon his mighty deeds aright — of Jim Crow, the elephant, the camel, the dromedaries, and the locomotive. Having expended his private fortune, on the two preceding days, in the purchase of the above unheard-of luxuries, the young gentleman's present errand was on the part of his mother, in quest of three eggs and half a pound of raisins. These articles Phœbe accordingly supplied, and, as a mark of gratitude for his previous patronage, and a slight superadded morsel after breakfast, put likewise into his hand a whale! The great fish, reversing his experience with the prophet of Nineveh, immediately began his progress down the same red pathway of fate whither so varied a caravan had preceded him. This remarkable urchin, in truth, was the very emblem of old Father Time, both in respect of his all-devour-

ing appetite for men and things, and because he,
as well as Time, after engulfing thus much of crea-
tion, looked almost as youthful as if he had been
just that moment made.

Not even so long a quotation as this can
give any fair idea of Hawthorne's humor, for,
graceful and delicate as it is, it has good
strong roots in all the preceding story. This
account of the visit of the little urchin to the
store is infinitely more full of humor if one has
read of his previous calls, of the establishing
of the store, and of the coming of Phœbe. Wit
can be quoted; but humor can never win jus-
tice from selections. One may learn half of
the multiplication-table and find it of occa-
sional service even if one does not know the
other half; but if you would get the full flavor
of a bit of humor in the works of Hawthorne

— and in those of any other author, for that matter — read the whole of the story.

The wit and humor of these authors are so interwoven with the serious and grave that no list of "humorous writings" can be given. Open the volumes of Holmes and Lowell almost anywhere, and you will soon come upon a flash of wit that will make you laugh, or a gleam of humor that will make you smile; and in Hawthorne you will find a humor even more graceful and delicate if not always so obvious. In Longfellow and Whittier the humor is less common, but it is so genuine that it is worth while to search for it.

HUMOR

QUESTIONS

1. Why are the stories from the "funny column" mentioned on page 3 utterly without humor?

   Because real humor is never unkind.

2. Who are our greatest poet-humorists?

   Lowell and Holmes.

3. Why are the "Biglow Papers" (Lowell, x., xi.) famous in the history of American humor?

   Because, save for the work of Irving, they are the earliest humorous books produced by an author of the first rank.

4. What is their language?

   The "Yankee dialect."

5. To what does the first series of "Biglow Papers" apply?

   To the Mexican War.

6. To what does the second series apply?
   To the Civil War.

7. To what does Lowell's "Jonathan to John"
   (x. 141) apply?
   *To the favor shown to the Confederates by
   British politicians.*

8. When was the "Atlantic Monthly" founded
   and in what is it unique?
   It was founded in 1857. *It is unique because during its life of more than half a
   century it has been purely literary.*

9. What is Holmes's best prose work?
   *The Breakfast-Table series: "The Auto-
   crat," "The Professor," and "The
   Poet"* (i., ii., iii.).

10. What two poems from these books are most
    famous and why?
    "The One-Hoss Shay" (xii. 417) *for its*

*humor; and "The Chambered Nauti-
lus" (xii. 393) for its loftiness of thought
and its beauty of expression.*

11. Why does "The Last Leaf" (xii. 3) deserve
to have been Lincoln's favorite?
*Because of its rare combination of humor
and the tenderest pathos.*

12. How does Lowell describe the humor of
Emerson?
*As playing "about the horizon of his mind
like heat-lightning."*

13. By what two qualities is Emerson's humor
marked?
*By a keen appreciation of the humorous
and a certain restraint in its expression.*

14. In which essays does he give his humor
most free rein?
*In those on "Mary Moody Emerson" (x.
397) and "Brook Farm" (x. 326).*

15. Which is his most humorous poem?

In his "Fable" (ix. 75), beginning, "The mountain and the squirrel."

16. Name two of Whittier's humorous poems.

"Abram Morison" (ii. 182) and "The Double-Headed Snake of Newbury" (i. 192).

17. Just where lies the humor in "The Courtship of Miles Standish" (ii. 299)?

In the refusal of the Captain to stand by his own motto.

18. Why has this poem always been a favorite?

Because it is so good a portrayal of friendship and honor, and because of its humor.

19. Of these six authors, whose humor is the most delicate?

Hawthorne.

20. Why is it more difficult to quote Hawthorne's humor than that of any other author?

HUMOR

Because its full flavor depends upon the context.

21. What does Lowell say of the difference between humor and wit?

   "*Humor may pervade a whole page without our being able to put our finger on any passage, and say 'It is here.' Wit must sparkle and snap in every line.*"

www.ingramcontent.com/pod-product-compliance
Lightning Source LLC
Chambersburg PA
CBHW052014240626
47153CB00008B/2876